W9-BAJ-257

INSIDE THE NFL

AFC NORTH

THE BALTIMORE RAVENS
THE CINCINNATI BENGALS
THE CLEVELAND BROWNS
THE PITTSBURGH STEELERS

BY BRIAN PETERSON

Published in the United States of America by
The Child's World® • 1980 Lookout Drive
Mankato, MN 56003-1705

800-599-READ • www.childsworld.com

ACKNOWLEDGEMENTS

The Child's World®: Mary Berendes,
Publishing Director

The Design Lab: Kathleen Petelinsek,
Design; Gregory Lindholm, Page Production

Manuscript consulting and photo research
by Shoreline Publishing Group LLC.

PHOTOS

Cover: Joe Robbins (front and back)
Interior: AP/Wide World: 5, 6, 9, 10, 15,
20, 24, 26, 28; Joe Robbins: 12, 13, 16,
19, 23, 27, 31, 32.

LIBRARY OF CONGRESS
CATALOGING-IN-PUBLICATION DATA

Peterson, Brian C.
  AFC North / by Brian Peterson.
    p. cm. — (Inside the NFL)
  Includes bibliographical references and index.
  ISBN 978-1-60253-002-7
(library bound : alk. paper)
  1. National Football League—History—Juvenile
literature. 2. Football—United States—History—
Juvenile literature. I. Title. II. Series.
  GV955.5.N35P47 2008
  796.332'640973—dc22   2008010520

Copyright © 2009 by The Child's World®.

All rights reserved. No part of this book may
be reproduced or utilized in any form or by any
means without written permission from the
publisher.

INTRODUCTION, 4

CHAPTER ONE
THE BALTIMORE RAVENS | 6

CHAPTER TWO
THE CINCINNATI BENGALS | 13

CHAPTER THREE
THE CLEVELAND BROWNS | 20

CHAPTER FOUR
THE PITTSBURGH STEELERS | 27

TIME LINE, 34

STAT STUFF, 36

GLOSSARY, 38

FIND OUT MORE, 39

INDEX, 40

AFC NORTH
INTRODUCTION

I n 2002, the National Football League (NFL) changed the way its teams are grouped. The league reorganized to eight **divisions** of four teams each. That created some new divisions, including the AFC (American Football Conference) North.

Among the teams in the AFC North are the Pittsburgh Steelers, whose five **Super Bowl** championships equal the most in NFL history. Pittsburgh's history dates back all the way to 1933.

The Cleveland Browns joined the NFL in 1950 after four years in the **rival** All-America Football Conference (AAFC). The Cincinnati Bengals began in a rival league, too: They were an **expansion team** in the American Football League (AFL) in 1968. Two years later, the Bengals and the nine other AFL teams joined the NFL.

The Baltimore Ravens are the youngest AFC North team. They did not officially come into being until the 1996 season. But by the 2000 season, they were Super Bowl champions.

In all, these four teams have racked up a total of 10 NFL titles. But their histories are much richer than just wins and losses, as you'll read in the upcoming chapters.

Cincinnati and Cleveland are Ohio neighbors. They battle twice each season in key AFC North games.

CHAPTER ONE

THE BALTIMORE RAVENS

 lthough the old Cleveland Browns moved to Baltimore in 1996 to become the Ravens, the NFL treats the Ravens as a new team. The history of the Browns remains with the new Browns team (see Chapter Three).

The fans in Baltimore were used to seeing NFL football. From 1953 to 1983, the Colts played there and became an important part of the city. After they moved to Indianapolis, fans desperately wished for a new team. Finally, in 1996, Cleveland Browns owner Art Modell moved his team to Baltimore. One of the reasons was that Baltimore promised to build Modell's team a new stadium.

At first, longtime Colts fans didn't like that their team was an "old" one from another city. But they soon warmed to the Ravens.

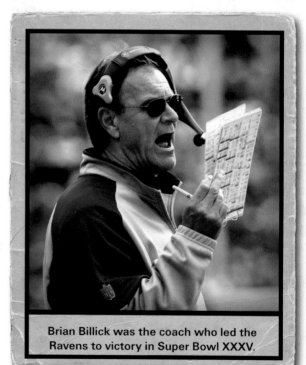

Brian Billick was the coach who led the Ravens to victory in Super Bowl XXXV.

The Ravens' new
stadium in 1998
originally was
called PSINet
Stadium, after
an Internet
company. Now,
Baltimore's home
is called M&T
Bank Stadium.

The first thing Modell needed was a name for his new team. The NFL decided that the name Browns would remain in Cleveland. A new Browns team would begin playing in 1999. Back in Baltimore, thousands of fans voted, and the winning name was Ravens. The name comes from a poem by Edgar Allan Poe, who lived in the city for much of his life. He wrote a famous poem in 1845 called "The Raven."

As with most new teams, the Ravens struggled in their early years. They had a losing record in each of their first three seasons (1996–98). A highlight for the team was the play of quarterback Vinny Testaverde. He was named to the **Pro Bowl** in 1996. Another big highlight came in 1998, when the team's new stadium opened.

After the Ravens finished just 6–10 in 1998, coach Ted Marchibroda was fired. The new coach was offensive-minded Brian Billick. This would prove to be Modell's smartest move since packing up for Baltimore.

In 1999, Billick's first season, the Ravens began to show sparks of success. Their powerful defense, led by linebacker Ray Lewis, allowed the third-fewest points in the NFC. Billick didn't make the offense into a powerhouse, but it was very much improved, and the team finished 8–8.

In 2000, the Ravens flew higher than ever before. While helping the team to a 12–4 record, the Lewis-led defense was ferocious. That defense allowed only 165 points, the fewest ever in a 16-game season. (NFL teams played 14 games in a season until 1978.) The Ravens shut out four teams, and they held seven other teams to 10 points or fewer.

"You don't know until you play us," Lewis said. "But our defense is like running into a buzz saw!"

The Ravens' offense that season was led by running back Jamal Lewis. He set a team record with 1,364 rushing yards, while scoring six touchdowns. A key part of Baltimore's success was also the kicking game. All-pro kicker Matt Stover led the AFL with 135 points, while Jermaine Lewis was a top punt returner.

The Ravens' defense led the way in the **playoffs.** Against Denver, Jamal Lewis scored twice, and the defense held the Broncos to a field goal. Ravens 21, Broncos 3. Facing division rival Tennessee next, Baltimore got help from all its parts. Jamal Lewis scored again, and Stover kicked a field goal. Anthony Mitchell returned a blocked field goal for another score, while Ray Lewis returned an **interception** 50 yards for a touchdown. Ravens 24, Titans 10.

In the AFC Championship Game, tight end Shannon Sharpe scored on a spectacular 96-yard catch from quarterback Trent Dilfer. Stover made three more field goals. And the defense was superb again: The Oakland Raiders managed only one field goal. Ravens 16, Raiders 3. Next stop: Super Bowl XXXV, against the NFC-champion New York Giants!

Once again, every part of the Ravens took part in the team's success. The defense led the way,

The Ravens' defense was incredible in the 2000 season. So it was fitting that linebacker Ray Lewis was named the MVP of the team's Super Bowl victory over the Giants.

Jamal Lewis was a punishing runner who didn't back down from any opposing tacklers.

allowing only 152 yards and no points. Baltimore intercepted four passes, with Duane Starks taking one in for a touchdown. Jermaine Lewis had a marvelous 84-yard kickoff return for a score. Dilfer

Jermaine Lewis returned a kickoff for a touchdown in the Ravens' win over the Giants in Super Bowl XXXV.

Defense has
been the name
of the game in
Baltimore. But
in 2003, Jamal
Lewis stood up
for the offense
by rushing for
2,066 yards.
That's the second-
highest single-
season total in
NFL history.

had a touchdown pass, while Jamal Lewis ran
for a score. The Giants scored only on a kickoff
return; otherwise, they came up empty. Ravens 34,
Giants 7. And Baltimore, once home to the NFL-
champion Colts, was once again home to football's
number-one team.

Baltimore fans were thrilled. Their hopes for a
football future flew back into town in 1996 on the
wings of a raven. Only four years later, the team
was a champion.

That Super Bowl season kicked off a great run
for the Ravens. They returned to the playoffs three
times in the next four seasons, plus they won a
division championship in 2003.

In 2004, Steven Bisciotti assumed complete
ownership of the team from Modell. After a couple
of so-so seasons, the team returned to the top
of the NFC North by winning a club-record 13
games during the regular season in 2006. That year
ended with a disappointing loss to eventual Super
Bowl-champion Indianapolis in the divisional
playoffs. Then the team slumped to a 5–11 record
in 2007, which cost Billick his job.

The new coach for 2008 was long-time
and highly regarded NFL assistant coach John
Harbaugh. He comes from a famous football
family. His dad, Jack Harbaugh, was a college
head coach. John's brother Jim is a former NFL
quarterback who is the current head coach at
Stanford University.

Harbaugh's hiring instantly brought a lot of
excitement to the Ravens. He inherited a defense

Star safety Ed Reed was the NFL's defensive player of the year in the 2004 season.

that remains the foundation of the team. That defense is led by Ray Lewis, who played his 12th season in Baltimore in 2007; Pro Bowl safety Ed Reed; and sack-happy linebacker Terrell Suggs.

CHAPTER TWO
THE CINCINNATI BENGALS

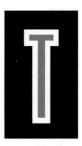he story of the Bengals is like a roller coaster—the team has reached terrific heights. But it also has plunged to depressing depths. At times, Cincinnati has been among football's best teams. More recently, the Bengals have bounced back and again look like they might be headed toward a spot among the AFC's best teams.

The roller-coaster ride began in 1968 when coach Paul Brown fielded the first Bengals team. In Cleveland, Brown was one of the NFL's greatest all-time coaches (see Chapter Three). He would not have as much success with Cincinnati, but his **reputation** helped the team get started.

Cincinnati played its first two seasons in the American Football League (AFL). The AFL combined with the NFL in 1970, and the Bengals joined the AFC

Paul Brown, a member of the Pro Football Hall of Fame, was the Bengals' first coach.

Central Division. They quickly made their mark by finishing the season with seven victories in a row. Their 8–6 record was the best in the AFC Central. Although they lost in the playoffs, it was a big step for a young team.

Paul Brown continued to show his football smarts by choosing a number of key players in the **draft.** In the coming years, those players would help the team almost reach the top of the NFL. Quarterback Ken Anderson was drafted in 1971, and wide receiver Isaac Curtis arrived two years later. In 1973, these young stars helped the Bengals win their second Central Division title.

Brown **retired** after the 1975 season, and the Bengals struggled for several years afterward. In 1980, however, they drafted a player who would become perhaps the best ever to wear the orange and black. Anthony Muñoz was a huge offensive lineman from the University of Southern California. With Cincinnati, he proved to be the key to the team's powerful offense. Opening holes for running backs and protecting Anderson, Muñoz started a career that would eventually send him to the Hall of Fame.

First, though, he helped the Bengals reach the Super Bowl. In 1981, Anderson led the NFL in passing, Muñoz made his first Pro Bowl, and Curtis was joined by Cris Collinsworth as key receivers. New coach Forrest Gregg had played with championship teams in Green Bay. He inspired the Bengals to reach the AFC Championship Game, where they faced an opponent tougher than

Paul Brown, formerly the highly successful coach of the Cleveland Browns, was inducted into the Pro Football Hall of Fame in 1967. The next season, he returned to the sidelines to coach the Bengals.

It was freezing in Cincinnati the day the Bengals beat the Chargers to win the 1981 AFC championship.

anything in a helmet: the weather. The game was played in Cincinnati in weather better for polar bears. The game-time temperature was minus-11 degrees (minus-24 C). The **windchill** made it feel like almost minus-60 (minus-51 C)! The Bengals overcame the terrible conditions to beat San Diego 27–7.

For six years in a row, beginning with the 1997 season, Corey Dillon ran for more than 1,000 yards.

In Super Bowl XVI, the Bengals lost to San Francisco, but their conference title was the team's finest moment to that date.

The team made the playoffs again in 1982, with Anderson setting an NFL record with a 70.55 completion percentage. The team struggled in the next few seasons, but in 1988, the Bengals came even closer to an NFL title. New quarterback Boomer Esiason, a left-

CINCINNATI BENGALS

Star defensive tackle Mike Reid was only 27 years old when he retired following the 1974 season. He wanted to pursue a country-music career. Reid went on to become a top songwriter in Nashville.

handed passer, was the NFL's most valuable player. Helped by the running back duo of James Brooks and Ickey Woods, Cincinnati finished with an all-time best record of 12–4. Woods became famous for his hopping, skipping post-touchdown dance. "The Ickey Shuffle" caught the attention of fans around the country.

After defeating the Buffalo Bills to win the AFC title, Ickey and the Bengals shuffled off to the Super Bowl. In Super Bowl XXIII, the Bengals faced the mighty San Francisco 49ers, led by legendary quarterback Joe Montana. The Bengals stunned the NFC champs by taking a 13–6 lead into the fourth quarter. The 49ers tied the score at 13–13, but then Cincinnati kicker Jim Breech made his third field goal of the game with less than four minutes left. The Bengals led 16–13 with little time remaining.

However, Montana was famous for his last-minute winning drives. He led the 49ers downfield against a desperate Bengals' defense. He completed a 10-yard touchdown pass to John Taylor with 34 seconds left to win the game. Once again, the Bengals were disappointed.

They would get used to that feeling in the next decade. From 1991 through 2002, the team never won more games than it lost in a season. The Bengals had some fine players in the 1990s, including quarterback Jeff Blake and receiver Carl Pickens. Running back Corey Dillon was perhaps the best player the team had since its Super Bowl days. Dillon made the Pro Bowl three years in a row from 1999 to 2001. In 2000, he set an NFL record (which has since been broken) by rushing for 278 yards in a single game.

In 2003, Ravens defensive coordinator Marvin Lewis was named the ninth head coach in Bengals' history. He helped to turn around the team's fortunes dramatically. In 2005, Cincinnati finished 11–5 and won the AFC North title.

Although Lewis was known for his defensive coaching ability, the Bengals have had some of the game's most dangerous offensive stars during his time. Quarterback Carson Palmer, the first player chosen overall in the 2003 draft, became the team's starting quarterback in 2004 and passed for more than 4,000 yards in 2006 and 2007—setting team records for passing yards in each season. Wide receiver Chad Johnson led the AFC in pass-catching yards each year from 2003 to 2006, then set a team record with 1,440 receiving yards in 2007. Fellow wideout T.J. Houshmandzadeh, who became the first player in Bengals' history to lead the NFL in receptions when he caught 112 passes in 2007, teams with Johnson to form one of the league's most dynamic pass-catching duos.

So far, Cincinnati has not been able to build on its division championship in 2005. The team missed the playoffs in both 2006 and 2007. But with Lewis continuing to improve the team's defense, and with the high-powered offense in full gear, the Bengals hope they can make the climb to the top of the roller coaster.

In 2005, former Bengals' star Ickey Woods became a head coach in Cincinnati. He took over as coach of the Cincinnati Sizzle in the National Women's Football Association.

The Bengals, including wide receiver Chad Johnson, hope they're on the road to new heights.

CHAPTER THREE

THE CLEVELAND BROWNS

The Cleveland Browns have been one of the most storied **franchises** in NFL history.

The team has won four NFL championships, and Cleveland also has been home to some of the game's greatest all-time players and the most vocal and loyal fans in the league.

Cleveland businessman Mickey McBride started the team in 1946 as part of a league called the All-America Football Conference (AAFC). He ran a contest in a newspaper to help pick a name for his new team. "Browns" won, in honor of their first coach. Paul Brown was not comfortable with having the team named after him, however. He suggested that perhaps it was a reference to boxing champion Joe Louis, who was known as the Brown Bomber. But no contest entries mentioned Louis.

Quarterback Otto Graham led the Browns to 10 championship games.

There were no
African-American
players in pro
football in the
mid-1940s. Paul
Brown helped
break the color
barrier by signing
Bill Willis and
Marion Motley
in 1946 to play
for his AAFC
team. He signed
them based on
their skills, not
the color of their
skin. The NFL's
Los Angeles
Rams also signed
two African-
American players
that same year.

Whether it was "his" team or not, Brown first made the Cleveland Browns a legendary team. The AAFC was around for only four seasons, and Cleveland won the championship every year. Brown brought many new developments to **professional** football. He was among the first coaches to study film of his opponents and to grade his players on their performance.

Brown also brought to the team some of the NFL's greatest all-time stars. Quarterback Otto Graham was a tough, solid player who did anything he needed to to make his team win. Graham led the Browns for 10 seasons, taking them to a title game every season. Running back Marion Motley was perhaps the hardest man to tackle in NFL history. Bill Willis and Lou Groza were Hall of Fame linemen.

The Browns and two other AAFC teams joined the NFL in 1950, and the older league challenged the new teams. They matched the Browns against the NFL-champion Philadelphia Eagles in the first game. The Browns stunned the NFL and the Eagles, winning easily 35–10. They continued to pound their NFL opponents all season, reaching the NFL Championship Game. Groza's 16-yard field goal with 28 seconds left gave the Browns the title over the Los Angeles Rams.

Although the Browns would reach the NFL title game in each of the next three seasons, they lost each game. In 1954, they made the championship game again. Before it began, Graham announced that it would be his last.

Inspired by their fearless leader, the Browns rolled to a 56–10 victory over the Lions. Graham had three touchdown passes and ran for three more scores. Brown eventually talked Graham into playing one more year, and the Browns won the league title again in 1955.

Two years later, another star joined the Browns. Jim Brown (no relation to Paul Brown) was an All-America running back, **lacrosse** star, and track champion. He burst into the league in 1957, winning **rookie** of the year honors and leading the league in rushing yards. He dominated the league for almost a decade, winning a record eight NFL rushing titles.

New owner Art Modell fired Coach Brown in 1962. In 1964, the new coach, Blanton Collier, relied on quarterback Frank Ryan and Jim Brown to lead Cleveland to the NFL championship. It would be the last time the Browns would either play for or win the league title.

Cleveland went through some down years in the 1970s. In 1980, however, the team's loyal fans were rewarded with a trip to the AFC playoffs. Quarterback Brian Sipe led the NFL in passing and was the league's most valuable player. But Sipe threw an interception in the end zone with less than a minute left, and the team lost the divisional playoffs. The Browns were disappointed again when they lost back-to-back conference title games to Denver in 1986 and 1987. The Browns suffered another loss to the Broncos in the 1989 AFC Championship Game.

In 1946, Otto Graham won championships in two different pro sports. In addition to leading football's Browns to the AAFC title, he also played for the National Basketball League-champion Rochester Royals that year.

Some experts consider Jim Brown the greatest running back in pro football history.

Through it all, Cleveland fans were becoming famous around the league. Some fans in end-zone seats began wearing dog masks and throwing dog-bone cookies onto the field. "The Dawg Pound" remains the NFL's most well-known group of football fanatics.

In 2007, Derek Anderson blossomed into a surprise star when he made the Pro Bowl.

In 1985, the Browns' Kevin Mack and Earnest Byner each ran for more than 1,000 yards. They became only the third set of teammates to reach that mark in the same season.

But in 1995, those fans were stunned when Modell announced late in the season that he was moving the team to Baltimore. It was a shock to a city that identified so closely with its team. The NFL promised to start another Browns team in the near future. That came in 1999, when a "new" Browns team started from scratch. The Browns of today keep all of the old Browns' records and colors and history. Unfortunately for the Dawg Pound, the new Browns have not yet matched the old Browns' record of success.

However, the new Browns are beginning to show a lot of promise. In 2002, the team made the playoffs as a **wild card,** but lost a heartbreaking game to division-rival Pittsburgh in the opening round. A couple of poor seasons followed before Romeo Crennel was hired as coach in 2005. Crennel had 25 years of NFL coaching experience and won three Super Bowls as defensive coordinator of the New England Patriots.

Following a pattern to success similar to the Patriots', Crennel built up the team gradually. In 2007, he guided the Browns to their best regular-season record (10–6) since the franchise restarted in 1999. Quarterback Derek Anderson passed for 3,787 yards and 29 touchdowns and was selected to the Pro Bowl. Running back Jamal Lewis, who signed as a **free agent** from Baltimore, rushed for 1,304 yards in 2007 and became only the 24th running back in league history to rush for more than 10,000 yards for his career. Those players, along with rising stars such as young wide receiver

In 2007, Braylon Edwards set Browns records for receiving yards (1,289) and touchdown catches (16).

Braylon Edwards, tight end Kellen Winslow, tackle Joe Thomas, and defensive tackles Shaun Rogers and Corey Williams, should provide a solid foundation that will help the Browns return among the NFL's top teams.

CHAPTER FOUR
THE PITTSBURGH STEELERS

As new NFL owners spend hundreds of millions of dollars to start their teams, it's amazing to remember that Pittsburgh businessman Art Rooney took his winnings ($2,500) from one day at the horse racetrack and purchased the Steelers in 1933. The Rooney family has turned that money into one of the most storied franchises in NFL history.

The Steelers are one of only three teams (the 49ers and the Cowboys are the others) in NFL history to win five Super Bowls. Their most recent NFL championship came in 2005 when, after starting the season with a 7–5 record, they won their final four games to make the playoffs. As a wild-card entry, the Steelers won three **consecutive** road games before defeating the Seattle Seahawks 21–10 in Super Bowl XL. Leading the charge for Pittsburgh was

Owner Art Rooney was popular with Steelers fans and players.

quarterback Ben Roethlisberger and wide receiver Hines Ward. Ward caught five passes for 123 yards and was named the game's most valuable player.

The Super Bowl victory capped one of the most exciting seasons in Steelers' history—and there have been a lot of them since the start of the franchise in 1933. That year, Pennsylvania's government legalized sports events on Sundays, and that's when Rooney saw the opening to buy an NFL franchise for Pittsburgh. He named his team the Pirates, after the local baseball team. After seven years without a winning record, the team changed its name to the Steelers in 1940. It didn't help; the Steelers still weren't very good.

During U.S. involvement in World War II (1941–1945), the entire NFL was smaller, as many of its players were in the **armed forces** in Europe or Asia. To keep playing in 1943, the Steelers combined with the Philadelphia Eagles and played one year as the "Steagles." In 1944, the Steelers mixed with the Chicago Cardinals as "Card-Pitt." After the war, the Steelers earned a playoff spot in 1947, but lost that game.

It was the last time they would be in the playoffs for more than two decades. The team was almost always on the bottom of the standings. To make matters worse, the Steelers cut future Hall of Fame quarterback Johnny Unitas in 1955. A couple of years later, they decided not to draft Jim Brown, who also turned out to be pretty good!

In 1969, Rooney hired a new coach. Under Chuck Noll, the Steelers turned from doormats

In 1975, Art Rooney turned the leadership of the Steelers over to his son Dan. In 2002, Dan placed the team's future in the hands of his son, Art Rooney II. Both Art Rooney I and Dan Rooney have been inducted into the Pro Football Hall of Fame.

Lynn Swann made this amazing catch in the Steelers' win over the Cowboys in Super Bowl X.

to champions. The key was Noll's ability to draft star players. Each year, the NFL holds a draft. Teams choose college players to join their team. From 1969 to 1974, Noll and the Steelers chose nine players who would eventually land in the Hall of Fame. Along the way, those players helped the Steelers win four Super Bowls.

The first piece of the puzzle was defensive tackle "Mean" Joe Greene, one of the best defensive players ever. Greene was soon joined by linebackers Jack Lambert and Jack Ham and cornerback Mel Blount. Pittsburgh's defense became known as the "Steel Curtain."

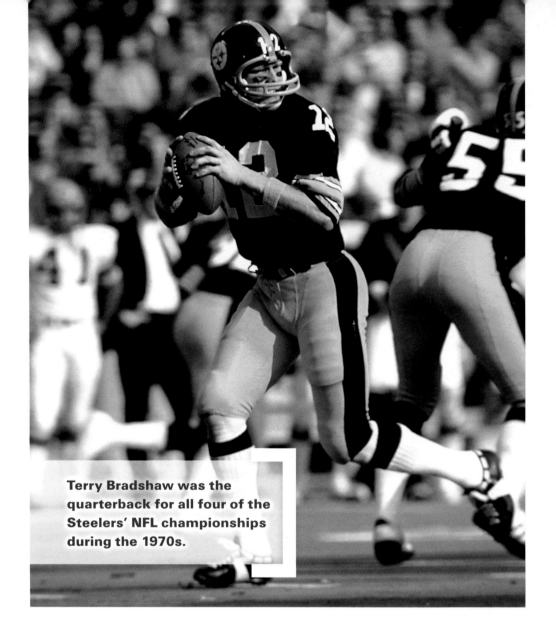

Terry Bradshaw was the quarterback for all four of the Steelers' NFL championships during the 1970s.

On offense, Noll chose quarterback Terry Bradshaw in 1970. A hard-throwing youngster from Louisiana, Bradshaw became an all-time great. He didn't start out that way, however. His first few seasons weren't very good. But Noll gave him some help with running back Franco Harris and receivers Lynn Swann and John Stallworth.

The team showed a flash of its future in 1972. The Steelers reached the playoffs for the first time since 1947. They played the Oakland Raiders and trailed late in the game, 7–6. Rooney was so

Multi-talented
Kordell Stewart
played for
Pittsburgh from
1995 to 2002. He
was nicknamed
"Slash" because
he was a
quarterback/
running back/
receiver (get it?).

sure the game was over, he took an elevator down to the field to congratulate the Raiders and console his players. While he was going down, he missed one of the wildest plays in NFL history.

Bradshaw dropped back to pass and **scrambled** around, looking for a receiver. He spotted Frenchy Fuqua downfield and fired a pass. Fuqua, Oakland's Jack Tatum, and the football all arrived at the same spot at the same time. The ball bounced backward, and Harris, trailing the play, caught it at his shoe tops. While the Pittsburgh fans went wild and the Raiders gave chase, Harris romped the final 42 yards of the winning 60-yard touchdown. The play would forever be known as the "Immaculate Reception."

Pittsburgh lost in the next round, but two years later, the Steelers finally reached a title game. They made the most of their chance. The Bradshaw-led offense and the Steel Curtain defeated Minnesota 16–6 in Super Bowl IX. Finally, after so many years of failure, Art Rooney owned a championship NFL team.

The Steelers repeated their title in Super Bowl X, defeating Dallas. They won again in Super Bowl XIII after the 1978 season. In Super Bowl XIV, they wrapped up an amazing run of four championships in six seasons. They were the first team to win four Super Bowls.

After the 1991 season—and with a couple more AFC Central Division titles to his credit— Noll retired. He was replaced by Cowher, who would remain the team's head coach through 2006.

Under Cowher, the Steelers were once again among the best teams. They earned six playoff spots in the 1990s. The highlight was their 1995 AFC championship. Although they lost to Dallas in Super Bowl XXX, they showcased one of the league's most multitalented players. Kordell Stewart was a rookie on that team, and he became the team's regular quarterback in 1996. He was also a good runner and caught several touchdown passes. Stewart's many talents helped the Steelers reach the AFC Championship Game after the 2001 season. They lost that game, but it was a sign of good things to come for the Steel City.

Coming off a 6–10 season in 2003, the Steelers chose a big, strong-armed quarterback in the draft. It proved to be an inspired choice. "Big Ben" Roethlisberger took over as the starter in the fifth week . . . and didn't lose for more than three months! He led the team to 13 consecutive victories, several of them in dramatic comebacks. The amazing rookie carried the team all the way back to the AFC Championship Game. They lost to the defending Super Bowl-champion New England Patriots, but the groundwork was in place for the Super Bowl championship in 2005.

The 2006 season was Cowher's 15th at the helm. After the year, he stepped down as coach. The next year, Mike Tomlin became only the third Steelers' coach in 39 seasons. Hiring an African-American head coach was particularly important to the Rooney family, who had worked for a greater presence of **minorities** among NFL leadership.

The 2004 Steelers were the first AFC team to win 15 games in the regular season. Pittsburgh's talent-filled roster included nine players who were selected to the Pro Bowl that year.

Wide receiver Hines Ward scored a touchdown on this play in Super Bowl XL. He was the game's MVP.

Tomlin was an immediate hit. In his first season as coach, the Steelers won 10 games and another AFC North championship. Roethlisberger passed for a club-record 32 touchdowns, and dynamic running back Willie Parker ran for more than 1,000 yards for the third season in a row. Wide receiver Santonio Holmes showed signs of becoming a big star, while safety Troy Polamalu keyed Pittsburgh's hard-hitting defense.

Although the season ended with a last-minute loss to the Jacksonville Jaguars in the wild-card round of the playoffs, Pittsburgh fans hope yet another Super Bowl championship is not far off.

TIME LINE

1933
Pittsburgh Steelers are founded

1974
Pittsburgh wins its first Super Bowl, beating Minnesota in game IX

1946
Cleveland Browns founded as part of the All-America Football Conference (AAFC)

1949
Browns win fourth AAFC title in the league's four years of existence

1940   1950   1960   1970

1950
Cleveland joins the NFL and wins the championship in its first season in the league

1954
Browns win first of back-to-back league titles

1964
Browns win their fourth NFL championship

1968
First season for the Cincinnati Bengals

1979
The Steelers beat the Rams in Super Bowl XIV to win the NFL title for the fourth time in six seasons

1981
The Bengals reach Super Bowl XVI, but lose to San Francisco

1988
The Bengals reach Super Bowl XXIII, but fall again to San Francisco

2000
Ravens win Super Bowl XXXV, beating the New York Giants

2002
NFC North is formed; Pittsburgh is the division's first champion

2005
Steelers win record-tying fifth Super Bowl, beating Seattle in game XL

1980

1990

2000

2010

1995
Pittsburgh reaches Super Bowl XXX before losing to Dallas

1996
Baltimore Ravens begin play after moving from Cleveland

1999
"New" Cleveland Browns begin play

STAT STUFF

TEAM RECORDS (THROUGH 2007)*

Team	All-time Record	Number of Titles (Most Recent)	Number of Times in Playoffs	Top Coach (Wins)
Baltimore	101–98–1	1 (2000)	4	Brian Billick (85)
Cincinnati	273–351–1	0	8	Sam Wyche (64)
Cleveland	435–380–10	4 (1964)	24	Paul Brown (115)
Pittsburgh	541–517–21	5 (2205)	24	Chuck Noll (209)

*includes AFL and NFL totals only

AFC NORTH CAREER LEADERS (THROUGH 2007)

Category	Name (Years With Team)	Total
Baltimore		
Rushing yards	Jamal Lewis (2000–06)	7,801
Passing yards	Vinny Testaverde (1996–97)	7,148
Touchdown passes	Vinny Testaverde (1996–97)	51
Receptions	Todd Heap (2001–07)	339
Touchdowns	Jamal Lewis (2000–06)	47
Scoring	Matt Stover (1996–2007)	1,342
Cincinnati		
Rushing yards	Corey Dillon (1997–2003)	8,061
Passing yards	Ken Anderson (1971–1986)	32,838
Touchdown passes	Ken Anderson (1971–1986)	197
Receptions	Chad Johnson (2001–07)	559
Touchdowns	Pete Johnson (1977–1983)	70
Scoring	Jim Breech (1980–1992)	1,151
Cleveland		
Rushing yards	Jim Brown (1957–1965)	12,312
Passing yards	Brian Sipe (1974–1983)	23,713
Touchdown passes	Brian Sipe (1974–1983)	154
Receptions	Ozzie Newsome (1978–1990)	662
Touchdowns	Jim Brown (1957–1965)	126
Scoring	Lou Groza (1950–59, 1961–67)	1,349
Pittsburgh		
Rushing yards	Franco Harris (1972–1983)	11,950
Passing yards	Terry Bradshaw (1970–1983)	27,989
Touchdown passes	Terry Bradshaw (1970–1983)	212
Receptions	Hines Ward (1998–2007)	719
Touchdowns	Franco Harris (1972–1983)	100
Scoring	Gary Anderson (1982–1994)	1,343

MEMBERS OF THE PRO FOOTBALL HALL OF FAME

Player	Position	Date Inducted
Baltimore		
None		
Cincinnati		
Charlie Joiner	Wide Receiver	1996
Anthony Muñoz	Tackle	1998
Cleveland		
Doug Atkins	Defensive End	1982
Jim Brown	Fullback	1971
Paul Brown	Coach	1967
Willie Davis	Defensive End	1981
Len Dawson	Quarterback	1987
Joe DeLamielleure	Guard	2003
Len Ford	Defensive End	1976
Frank Gatski	Center	1985
Otto Graham	Quarterback	1965
Lou Groza	Tackle/Kicker	1974
Gene Hickerson	Guard	2007
Henry Jordan	Defensive Tackle	1995
Leroy Kelly	Running Back	1994
Dante Lavelli	End	1975
Mike McCormack	Tackle	1984
Tommy McDonald	Wide Receiver	1998
Bobby Mitchell	Wide Receiver/Running Back	1983
Marion Motley	Fullback	1968
Ozzie Newsome	Tight End	1999
Paul Warfield	Wide Receiver	1983
Bill Willis	Middle Guard	1977
Pittsburgh		
Bert Bell	Owner	1963
Mel Blount	Cornerback	1989
Terry Bradshaw	Quarterback	1989
Len Dawson	Quarterback	1987
Bill Dudley	Halfback	1966
Joe Greene	Defensive Tackle	1987
Jack Ham	Linebacker	1988
Franco Harris	Running Back	1990
Robert "Cal" Hubbard	Tackle	1963
John Henry Johnson	Fullback	1987
Walt Kiesling	Guard/Coach	1966
Jack Lambert	Linebacker	1990
Bobby Layne	Quarterback	1967
Johnny (Blood) McNally	Halfback	1963
Marion Motley	Fullback	1968
Chuck Noll	Coach	1993
Art Rooney	Owner	1964
Dan Rooney	Owner	2000
John Stallworth	Wide Receiver	2002
Ernie Stautner	Defensive Tackle	1969
Lynn Swann	Wide Receiver	2001
Mike Webster	Center	1997

OSSARY

armed forces—the military

consecutive—in a row, one after the other

divisions—in the NFL, teams are placed in one of these four-team groups

draft—held each April, this is when NFL teams choose college players to join their teams; the teams with the worst records the prior season choose first, but draft picks can be traded to move a team's draft order

expansion team—a new team that starts from scratch

franchises—more than just the teams, they are the entire organizations that are members of a professional sports league

free agent—a player who has completed his contract with one team and is free to sign with any other team

inducted—to become a member of a group or club

interception—when a defensive player catches a pass thrown by the offense

lacrosse—a field sport in which players use long sticks with basket ends to throw and catch a ball; goals are scored by throwing the ball into a net

minorities—in this case, people who are African American, Hispanic American, or Asian American

playoffs—after the regular schedule, these are the games played to determine the champion

Pro Bowl—the NFL's annual all-star game

professional—someone who is paid to perform an activity (in this case, play football)

reputation—how a person is thought of by other people

retired—left a job after a long period of service

rival—someone who competes for the same goal

rookie—an athlete in his or her first season as a professional

roster—the list of players on a team

scrambled—when a quarterback runs around looking for an open receiver or makes a run past the line of scrimmage himself

Super Bowl—the NFL's annual championship game, played in late January or early February at a different stadium each year

wild card—a team that makes the playoffs without winning a division title

windchill—a measurement of temperature that combines the air temperature with the wind speed

FIND OUT MORE

Books

Frederick, Sara, and Sara Gilbert. *The History of the Cincinnati Bengals.* Mankato, Minn.: Creative Education, 2004.

Frederick, Sara, and Sara Gilbert. *The History of the Cleveland Browns.* Mankato, Minn.: Creative Education, 2004.

Ladewski, Paul. *National Football League Superstars 2007.* New York: Scholastic, 2007.

Marini, Matt. *Football Top 10.* New York: DK Publishing, 2002.

Nichols, John. *The History of the Baltimore Ravens.* Mankato, Minn.: Creative Education, 2005.

Stewart, Mark. *The Pittsburgh Steelers.* Chicago: Norwood House Press, 2006.

Zuehlke, Jeffrey. *Ben Roethlisberger.* Minneapolis, Minn.: First Avenue Editions, 2007.

On the Web

Visit our Web site for lots of links about the AFC North: *http://www.childsworld.com/links*

Note to Parents, Teachers, and Librarians: We routinely verify our Web links to make sure they are safe, active sites—so encourage your readers to check them out!

INDEX

Anderson, Derek, 24, 25
Anderson, Ken, 14, 16

Billick, Brian, 6, 7, 11
Bisciotti, Steven, 11
Blake, Jeff, 17
Blount, Mel, 29
Bradshaw, Terry, 30, 31
Breech, Jim, 17
Brooks, James, 17
Brown, Jim, 22, 23, 28
Brown, Paul, 13, 14, 20–21, 22
Byner, Earnest, 25

Collier, Blanton, 22
Collinsworth, Cris, 14
Cowher, Bill, 31–32
Crennel, Romeo, 25
Curtis, Isaac, 14

Dilfer, Trent, 8, 9, 11
Dillon, Corey, 16, 17–18

Edwards, Braylon, 26
Esiason, Boomer, 16–17

Fuqua, Frenchy, 31

Graham, Otto, 20, 21, 22
Greene, Joe "Mean Joe", 29
Gregg, Forrest, 14–15
Groza, Lou, 21

Ham, Jack, 29
Harbaugh, Jack, 11
Harbaugh, Jim, 11
Harbaugh, John, 11
Harris, Franco, 30, 31
Holmes, Santonio, 33
Houshmandzadeh, T. J., 18

Johnson, Chad, 18, 19

Lambert, Jack, 29
Lewis, Jamal, 8, 9, 11, 25
Lewis, Jermaine, 8, 9, 10
Lewis, Martin, 18
Lewis, Ray, 7, 8, 12
Louis, Joe, 20

Mack, Kevin, 25
Marchibroda, Ted, 7
McBride, Mickey, 20
Mitchell, Anthony, 8
Modell, Art, 6, 7, 11, 22, 25
Montana, Joe, 17
Motley, Marion, 21
Muñoz, Anthony, 14

Noll, Chuck, 28–29, 30, 31

Palmer, Carson, 18
Parker, Willie, 33
Pickens, Carl, 17
Polamalu, Troy, 33

Reed, Ed, 12
Reid, Mike, 17
Roethlisberger, "Big Ben", 28, 32, 33
Rogers, Shaun, 26
Rooney, Art, 27, 28, 30–31, 32
Ryan, Frank, 22

Sharpe, Shannon, 8
Sipe, Brian, 22
Stallworth, John, 30
Starks, Duane, 9
Stewart, Kordell "Slash", 31, 32
Stover, Matt, 8
Suggs, Terrell, 12
Swann, Lynn, 29, 30

Tatum, Jack, 31
Taylor, John, 17
Testaverde, Vinny, 7
Thomas, Joe, 26
Tomlin, Mike, 32–33

Unitas, Johnny, 28

Ward, Hines, 28, 33
Williams, Corey, 26
Willis, Bill, 21
Winslow, Kellen, 26
Woods, Ickey, 17, 18